WELCOME TO MY COUNTRY

Welcome to
SINGAPORE

Gareth Stevens Publishing
A WORLD ALMANAC EDUCATION GROUP COMPANY

Written by
**YONG JUI LIN/JAMES MICHAEL BAKER
& JUNIA MARION BAKER**

Edited in USA by
DOROTHY L. GIBBS

Designed by
GEOSLYN LIM

Picture research by
SUSAN JANE MANUEL

First published in North America in 2003 by
Gareth Stevens Publishing
A World Almanac Education Group Company
330 West Olive Street, Suite 100
Milwaukee, Wisconsin 53212 USA

Please visit our web site at:
www.garethstevens.com
For a free color catalog describing
Gareth Stevens' list of high-quality
books and multimedia programs,
call 1-800-542-2595 (USA) or
1-800-387-3178 (CANADA).
Gareth Stevens Publishing's fax: (414) 332-3567.

© **TIMES MEDIA PRIVATE LIMITED 2003**
Originated and designed by
Times Editions
An imprint of Times Media Private Limited
A member of the Times Publishing Group
Times Centre, 1 New Industrial Road
Singapore 536196
http://www.timesone.com.sg/te

Library of Congress Cataloging-in-Publication Data
Yong, Jui Lin.
Welcome to Singapore/ Yong Jui Lin, James Michael Baker, and
Junia Marion Baker.
p. cm. — (Welcome to my country)
Includes bibliographical references and index.
Summary: An overview of the geography, history, government,
economy, people, and culture of Singapore.
ISBN 0-8368-2546-2 (lib. bdg.)
1. Singapore—Juvenile literature. [1. Singapore.]
I. Baker, James Michael. II. Baker, Junia Marion. III. Title. IV. Series.
DS609.Y66   2003
959.57—dc21   2002030339

Printed in Malaysia

1 2 3 4 5 6 7 8 9 07 06 05 04 03

Contents

Words that appear in the glossary are printed in **boldface** type the first time they occur in the text.

Welcome to Singapore!

The Republic of Singapore has grown from a small nineteenth-century trading post to a major global business center. Even without any **natural resources**, this tiny nation offers the highest **living standard** in Southeast Asia. Let's visit Singapore and its hardworking people.

Opposite: Built in the 1920s, Elgin Bridge crosses the Singapore River not far from the Central Business District.

Below: From designer clothing to arts and antiques, Singapore is a great place to shop.

The Flag of Singapore

Singapore's flag is red and white. Red stands for brotherhood and equality, white for virtue and purity. The crescent moon and five stars on the red band symbolize a young nation of peace, progress, equality, justice, and democracy.

The Land

Singapore's total area of 255 square miles (660 square kilometers) includes a main island and about sixty **adjacent** islands. From east to west, the distance across the main island is about 26 miles (42 kilometers). From north to south, the distance is about 14 miles (23 km). To the north, the Johor **Strait** separates the main island from the peninsula of Malaysia. To the south, the Singapore

Below: Villagers on some offshore islands, such as Pulau Seking, still lead rural lifestyles.

Strait separates it from the islands
of Indonesia. The South China Sea
lies along its eastern coast.

Much of Singapore's land is flat,
rarely rising over 50 feet (15 meters)
above sea level. The highest point, at
545 feet (166 m), is Bukit Timah Hill.
Populated areas take up about half of
the land, and about 5 percent is rain
forest or mangrove swamps. The rest
has parks, green space, and open areas.

Above:
Narrow footpaths
in the Bukit Timah
Nature Reserve
are popular hiking
trails in central
Singapore.

Climate

Located only 85 miles (137 km) north of the equator, Singapore has a tropical climate. It is hot and **humid** all year. Average daily temperatures are 73° to 93° Fahrenheit (23° to 34° Celsius), and rain falls throughout the year. The country's two main seasons are the northeast **monsoon** from December to March and the southwest monsoon from June to September.

Above:
More than seven hundred kinds of orchids grow in Singapore's hot, humid climate. The country's national flower is an orchid called the Vanda Miss Joaquim.

Plants and Animals

Over three thousand kinds of tropical plants keep Singapore lush and green. Most of them grow in the country's mangrove swamps and nature reserves. Flowering plants, such as orchids and bougainvillea, grow as easily as the tropical hardwood and coconut trees. Angsana, pulai, frangipanni, and rain trees are also common in Singapore.

The wildlife of Singapore is limited to mainly birds, frogs, and snakes, with some monkeys and squirrels in forest areas. The country has about 150 kinds of birds, and another 100 bird species **migrate** there twice a year.

Below: Zebras and many other kinds of animals enjoy the natural habitats re-created for them at the Singapore Zoological Gardens.

History

Long ago, Singapore was called *Temasek* (tuh-MAH-sek), which means "sea town." By the end of the fourteenth century, it was more commonly known as *Singapura,* a **Sanskrit** word that means "lion city."

Englishman Sir Thomas Stamford Raffles, who was a representative of the **East India Company** (EIC), founded modern Singapore in 1819. Although the country then belonged to the Dutch, Raffles convinced a

Below: One of Singapore's early settlers, the *Orang Laut* (OH-rahng LAH-oat) were sea gypsies who lived on houseboats.

chief of the territory to appoint a ruler who was friendly to the British and would turn Singapore over to the EIC. The country **prospered** under EIC rule, but crime was widespread. In 1867, the British government took Singapore away from the EIC.

With the opening of the Suez Canal in 1869, trade between Europe and Asia flourished. Because of its central location, Singapore became a key port. Today, it is the world's seventh largest.

Above: A statue of Sir Thomas Stamford Raffles stands at the spot along the Singapore River where Raffles was thought to have landed in 1819.

Toward Independence

During World War II, the Japanese occupied Singapore from 1942 to 1945. The surrender of British forces showed the people of Singapore that Britain was not an unbeatable world power, and many Asian Singaporeans started thinking about self-rule. After the war, however, the British returned.

By the 1950s, most Singaporeans wanted Britain to give up power. The first step toward independence came in 1955, when David Saul Marshall

Above: After World War II, the people of Singapore gladly welcomed back the British. Very soon, however, they were asking for self-rule.

became the first locally elected chief minister. Marshall resigned in 1956, but the next chief minister, Lim Yew Hock, worked out an agreement with Britain to create the State of Singapore. In 1959, Lee Kuan Yew's People's Action Party won the first elections.

Singapore became independent from Britain in 1963, joining the Federation of Malaya to form the new country of Malaysia. When disagreements ended this union in 1965, Singapore became the independent Republic of Singapore.

Left: Goh Chok Tong succeeded Lee Kuan Yew as Singapore's prime minister in 1990. Both belong to the People's Action Party, which won the country's first state elections and has been in power ever since.

The Struggle for Success

The new republic had many problems, including few natural resources and, since British military bases closed in 1971, no defense forces. In addition, housing and unemployment problems created tension and violence among the country's **multicultural** population. Modern Singapore shows tremendous progress in changing these situations and building a strong national identity.

Below: Singapore's busy Central Business District reflects a society willing to work hard for the nation's interests and create a stable country with a healthy economy.

Elizabeth Choy (1910–)

During World War II, Elizabeth Choy, who came to Singapore in 1929 to teach, was held prisoner and tortured by the Japanese. They accused her of helping the Allies sabotage Japanese ships. She received the Order of the British Empire award for her heroism.

Elizabeth Choy

Yusof bin Ishak (1910–1970)

In 1959, when Singapore had limited self-rule, Yusof bin Ishak became the first Malayan-born head of state. In 1965, he became the first president of the Republic. With his commitments to both equality and education, he set a good example for future leaders.

Yusof bin Ishak

David Saul Marshall (1908–1995)

A brilliant lawyer and public speaker, David Saul Marshall inspired many Singaporeans to join their country's struggle for independence. In 1955, he became Singapore's first locally elected chief minister.

David Saul Marshall

Government and the Economy

Singapore is a **city-state**, so it does not have a system of local governments, and the national government is actively involved in city matters. The nation's one-house parliament is advised by a president, who is elected by the people. Members of Parliament are also elected. The prime minister is a member who represents the majority party.

Above: Lee Kuan Yew was Singapore's prime minister from 1959 to 1990 and is still active in Parliament.

Left: Singapore's new Parliament House was built in 1999. It houses the cabinet, which is led by the prime minister and is responsible for all government administration.

Singapore's government considers housing, education, and social welfare very important matters. Employers and employees make monthly payments to the Central Provident Fund (CPF) for savings and retirement. People can use their CPF money for medical, housing, and advanced education needs. Schools, hospitals, and other public services are supported by the government.

Above: Areas in Singapore known as housing estates have both offices and homes in them. Directly behind this office building is an apartment building, constructed under Singapore's public housing program.

The Economy

Modern Singapore is one of the richest countries in the world. It is a global center for manufacturing, finance, and communication. Since 1965, when the country became independent, its economy has grown rapidly. At first, the focus was on industry. Then, in the 1970s and 1980s, Singapore became more active in business and financial services. Manufacturing, however, is still the main economic activity.

Above: A central location along international trade routes has made Singapore's ports among the busiest in the world.

The government of Singapore spends large amounts of money to maintain world-class services and facilities, including its seaports and Changi International Airport. After New York, London, and Tokyo, the nation ranks fourth largest as a center for banking and finance.

To stay competitive in the twenty-first century, Singapore encourages the growth of technology business **ventures** and has been shifting to a more knowledge-based economy.

Above: Tourism is a major part of the island's economy.

Below: Singapore Airlines is one of the most profitable in the world.

People and Lifestyle

Most of Singapore's population is Chinese. Malays and Indians are two other main **ethnic groups**. Almost a million foreigners live and work in Singapore, too.

For quality of life, based on income, education, and how long people live, Singapore is one of the world's top ten countries.

Left: Family time is very important to the people of Singapore. In over 75 percent of the nation's families, both parents work outside the home.

Employment and Housing

Almost 60 percent of Singapore's people have jobs, and unemployment is very low. Singaporeans work hard, usually at least forty-four hours a week.

Thanks to government programs, most people in Singapore own their homes. About 90 percent live in high-rise apartments built by the Housing and Development Board (HDB) in areas known as housing estates.

Above:
Singaporeans look forward to special occasions spent with family and friends.

Family Life

Several generations of family members living in the same house is common in Singapore. Because, in many families, both parents work, grandparents often live in the same household to help raise their grandchildren. Parents depend on other relatives, too, as well as on maids and child care centers, for help with the children. Some parents spend time with their children only on weekends.

Above:
The traditional Malay wedding ceremony, known as the *akad nikah* (AH-kahd NEE-kah), is a spoken contract between the groom and the bride's father. To complete the ceremony, the groom gives his bride money.

Most families have only one or two children. Although very spoiled, children are expected, even at a young age, to measure up to high standards, especially to be successful in school. They often have private tutors to help improve their grades.

On weekends, when most parents are not working, the whole family goes shopping, works on household chores, or enjoys leisure activities together.

Below: Singaporean children may be pampered, but they are also pressured, from a young age, to be successful.

Education

Singapore has one of the world's best education systems. Singaporeans see education as the key to a successful life, so, even as adults, they continue taking classes to upgrade their skills.

Starting at age six, children must attend six years of elementary school. Then, most go on to four or five years of high school. Courses include the study of English as well as a language related to the student's **native tongue**.

Below:
Today, more and more students in Singapore are learning some of their lessons on a computer.

Left: About sixty thousand students attend Singapore's four polytechnics. The coursework offered at these schools focuses on engineering, business, and information technology.

Higher Education

For education beyond high school, Singapore has three universities and four polytechnics. The country also has many private institutions that offer distance education with foreign universities, which is a good way for working adults to continue learning. Most of the foreign universities are based in the United States, the United Kingdom, and Australia.

Religion

The people of Singapore have freedom of religion, and over three-quarters of the population follows a religion. Since most Singaporeans are Chinese, about 50 percent of the people are Buddhists. About 15 percent, mostly Malays, are Muslims, and another 15 percent are Christians, a third of whom are Roman Catholics. Slightly more than 3 percent are Hindus, almost all of whom are from India or are of Indian heritage.

Above: Buddhists in Singapore honor both Buddha and **Confucius.** These women are making an offering at a Buddhist temple.

Singapore honors its many religions by observing national holidays for each ethnic group. *Vesak* (VAY-sahk) Day **commemorates** the birth of Buddha. The Christian holidays Christmas and Good Friday represent the birth and death of Jesus Christ.

Besides having religious holidays, Singapore's Muslims and Hindus have their own councils to advise the nation's government regarding issues that affect their religions.

Left:
The beautifully carved statues of Hindu gods and goddesses found in Singapore's temples are usually the work of skilled Indian craftsmen.

Language

English, Mandarin (Chinese), Malay, and Tamil (Indian) are Singapore's four official languages. Malay, which was spoken by the region's earliest settlers, is its national language. English took over as the language of business when Singapore was a British colony and, since the 1960s, has become the main language. Most Chinese Singaporeans speak both English and Mandarin.

Left: Because the population of Singapore has so many ethnic groups, many signs include more than one language.

Literature

Although the countries of its various ethnic groups have given Singapore a rich literary history, Singaporeans usually consider works produced since 1965, the year of independence, as their nation's literature. One of Singapore's best known authors is Catherine Lim (1942–). Other well-known writers include poet Goh Poh Seng (1936–) and playwright Kuo Pao Kun (1939–).

Above: Reading is a popular pastime for people riding Singapore's rapid transit trains.

Below: Catherine Lim writes short stories and novels.

Arts

A National Arts Council in Singapore encourages all forms of art, both local and international. It sponsors writing and music competitions as well as the month-long annual Singapore Arts Festival. A huge new performing arts center, Esplanade Theatres on the Bay, has been built to house a variety of arts. It includes five auditoriums, as well as several outdoor performance spaces.

Below:
This building was once a high school for boys that was run by Christian missionaries. Now it is the Singapore Art Museum.

Visual Arts

The Singapore Art Museum features **contemporary** Southeast Asian Art, particularly by Singaporean artists. The country's visual artists have also organized cultural exchanges showing local artwork overseas. Georgette Chen (1906–1993), one of Singapore's pioneer artists; sculptor Ng Eng Teng (1934–2001); and watercolor painter Ong Kim Seng (1945–) have all held international exhibitions.

Above:
Since 1987, this sculpture has been an identifying landmark outside the Singapore History Museum. It is part of a series called "The Living World," by Taiwanese artist Ju Ming.

Architecture

Traditional forms of architecture can still be found among Singapore's skyscrapers and shopping malls. The National Heritage Board has saved many old buildings from being torn down, including Chinatown's pre-World War II **shophouses**. Also, some architects are trying to design new buildings with elements of older Asian and colonial architectural styles.

Above: Some of Singapore's old shophouses have been restored to their original style. Many of them are now restaurants or offices.

Music and Theater

The annual Singapore International Jazz Festival always draws crowds. The country also has internationally known musicians who have performed with the Singapore Symphony Orchestra.

Chinese, Malay, Indian, and English theater groups all play important roles in Singapore's active performing arts scene. Plays deal with Asian problems as well as with love, life, and death.

Below: Ballet is a particularly popular form of dance in Singapore. Along with classical and modern dance, it is part of the work of the Singapore Dance Theatre, which was founded in 1988. Ballet lessons are even given in some Singapore schools.

Leisure

Singapore has a great variety of food, and almost every leisure activity also includes eating. Popular activities are everything from flower arranging to line dancing to outdoor sports, such as golf, cycling, swimming, and jogging. Community clubs across the country organize many of the activities. Teens like to play computer games and hang out with friends at shopping malls.

Below: Singaporeans enjoy eating out, particularly on weekends. Dining at a restaurant or a food court gives them a chance to visit with family and friends.

Left: Computers and information technology are important parts of everyday life in Singapore. From an early age, children are encouraged to play computer games and to surf the Internet.

Many Singaporeans like to take day trips to Malaysia. Although close to each other, the two countries are very different, and Malaysia's resort areas give Singapore visitors a sense of space.

At home, the people of Singapore like to watch television, listen to the radio, read, play computer games, and surf the Internet. Over half of all homes in Singapore have Internet access.

Left: Soccer and track and field are the most popular sports for students in Singapore. Soccer is played mostly by boys, but boys and girls, by the thousands, participate in track and field events.

Sports

While soccer is Singapore's favorite spectator sport, the nation promotes participation in sports as a healthy way of life. The Singapore Sports Council's "Sports for Life" program organizes fitness events, such as walkathons and swimming competitions, on a national level, and many of Singapore's housing estates have sports facilities, including swimming pools, tennis courts, and even stadiums, for public use.

Above: Weightlifter Tan Howe Liang is Singapore's only Olympic athlete, so far, to win a medal. He won a silver medal at the Rome Olympics in 1960.

International Competitions

When competing with other countries, Singapore has been the most successful in swimming. In the 1990s, national swimmers Joscelin Yeo and Ang Peng Siong both broke records in the Southeast Asian (SEA) Games. Singaporean athletes have also done well in Ping-Pong and bowling events in the SEA Games and the Asian Games.

Below: At the biennial Southeast Asian Games, Singapore's water polo team has won eighteen gold medals in a row.

Ethnic Festivals

With its multicultural population, Singapore has many ethnic festivals and holidays. Because most of the people are Chinese, the most widely celebrated holiday is the Chinese New Year, in January or February. The festival begins with a family reunion dinner and includes fifteen more days of feasting and visiting.

Above:
Chinatown is a popular place to shop for Chinese New Year gifts and decorations. Small red envelopes with money inside them, called *hong bao* (HUNG-bough), are traditional gifts for children.

The Indian community of Singapore celebrates Hindu festivals, including *Deepavali* (dee-PAHV-ah-lee), or the Festival of Lights, which honors the triumph of good over evil.

The Muslim holiday *Hari Raya Puasa* (HAH-ree RYE-ah PWAH-sah) celebrates the end of Ramadan (RAH-mah-dahn), Islam's month of **fasting**.

Above: Dragon and lion dances are performed in Singapore to bring good luck.

Left: During their *Thaipusam* (TIE-poo-sahm) festival, Hindus carry huge headdresses called *kavadis* (KAH-vah-dees), which hold offerings of fruits, flowers, and milk.

Food

Food is one of Singapore's greatest attractions. The country's many ethnic groups contribute to an **exotic** variety of **cuisines**. Chinese dishes, which are typically eaten with chopsticks, range from delicate Cantonese to hot, spicy Szechuan. Most Malay dishes are made with coconut milk, chilies, and other spices. South Indian meals are usually vegetables or lentils with rice.

Above: The prickly-skinned durian is an exotic tropical fruit that is known in Singapore as the king of fruits.

Left: Fried, flat noodles called *char kway teow* (CHAR kway tee-ow) are a popular food sold at both street stalls and restaurants in Singapore.

North Indian *vindaloo* (VIN-dah-loo) is a hot tomato and chicken or lamb stew, eaten with rice and a cucumber-herb yogurt. Malay and Indian diners eat with forks and spoons but, at times, prefer to use only their right hands.

Because meals in Singapore are so rich and spicy, desserts tend to be simple and refreshing, such as fresh fruits, gelatins, or puddings.

Above:
Singaporeans eat out a lot, so the restaurants, food courts, and street stalls all serve international as well as local foods.

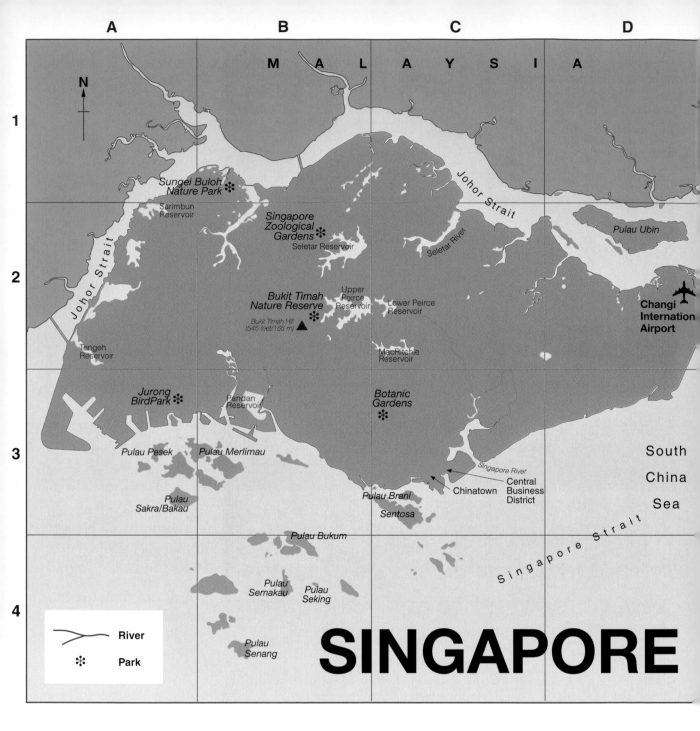

A B C D

MALAYSIA

1

N

Sungei Buloh
Nature Park ❊

Sarimbun
Reservoir

Singapore
Zoological
Gardens ❊

Seletar Reservoir

Johor Strait

Seletar River

Pulau Ubin

Changi
Internation
Airport

2

Bukit Timah
Nature Reserve

Upper
Peirce
Reservoir

Lower Peirce
Reservoir

Johor Strait

Bukit Timah Hill
(545 feet/166 m) ▲ ❊

Tengeh
Reservoir

MacRitchie
Reservoir

Jurong
BirdPark ❊

Pandan
Reservoir

Botanic
Gardens
❊

3

Pulau Pesek

Pulau Merlimau

Singapore River

Chinatown

Central
Business
District

South

China

Sea

Pulau
Sakra/Bakau

Pulau Brani

Sentosa

Pulau Bukum

Singapore Strait

Pulau
Semakau

Pulau
Seking

4

River

❊ Park

Pulau
Senang

SINGAPORE

Above: Singapore's Botanic Gardens attracts over two million visitors every year.

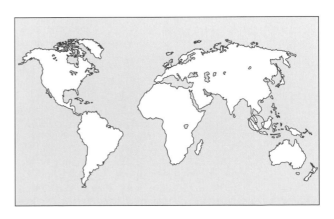

Quick Facts

Official Name Republic of Singapore

Official Languages Mandarin (Chinese), English, Malay, Tamil (Indian)

Population 4,452,732 (2002 estimate) *About 1,000,000 are not citizens or permanent residents.*

Land Area 255 square miles (660 square km)

Highest Point Bukit Timah Hill 545 feet (166 m)

Main Ethnic Groups Chinese, Malay, Indian

Major Religions Buddhist, Muslim, Christian, Hindu

Important Holidays Chinese New Year (January/February)

 Good Friday (March/April)

 Vesak Day (May)

 National Day (August 9)

 Deepavali (October/November)

 Christmas (December 25)

 Hari Raya Puasa (December/January)

Currency Singapore dollar (S$ 1.73 = U.S. $1 as of 2002)

Opposite: Masks of characters from Chinese mythology are popular souvenirs.

Glossary

adjacent: next to or nearby.

city-state: a single city that has the political power of a nation, such as ancient Rome or Athens.

commemorates: remembers or calls to mind; honors with a special ceremony.

Confucius: an ancient Chinese teacher and philosopher whose ideas about moral character and responsibility have greatly influenced Chinese society throughout history.

contemporary: recent or present-day.

cuisines: distinct and specialized styles of preparing and cooking foods.

East India Company: a major shipping business in England that controlled a large part of the trade with the Far East in the 1700s and 1800s.

ethnic groups: collections of people within a larger society who share a common culture, race, or national heritage and often the same language, religion, or way of life.

exotic: unusual and often unfamiliar because it is from a different country.

fasting: going without food or drink, often for religious reasons.

humid: damp, usually describing the amount of moisture in the air.

living standard: the least amount of necessities and comforts considered customary and essential for the people of a particular society or region.

migrate: move from one country, region, or location to another.

monsoon: a strong, seasonal wind that sometimes brings heavy rains.

multicultural: having many cultures or ethnic groups within a single society.

native tongue: the language of a person's birthplace or the country or region of his or her ancestry.

natural resources: materials existing or produced in nature that are valuable and useful to human societies.

prospered: succeeded or grew in a rapid or forceful way.

Sanskrit: the ancient language of India.

shophouses: historic two-story structures built by Chinese immigrants, which had a business on the lower level and housed the business owner's family on the upper level.

strait: a narrow strip of sea between two masses of land, which joins two larger bodies of water.

ventures: activities that involve risk or uncertainty.

More Books to Read

Buddhist Temple. Places of Worship series. Angela Wood (Gareth Stevens)

Chopsticks for My Noodle Soup: Eliza's Life in Malaysia. Susan E. Goodman (Millbrook Press)

A Family in Singapore. Bridget Goom (Lerner)

Fun with Chinese Festivals. Tan Huay Peng (Federal Publications)

Malaysia in Pictures. Visual Geography series. Department of Geography (Lerner)

A Photographic Guide to Birds of Peninsular Malaysia and Singapore. G. W. H. Davison and Chew Yen Fook (Chelsea Green)

Singapore. Dorling Kindersley Travel Guides. Jill A. Laidlaw, *et al* (DK Publishing)

Singapore. Faces and Places series. Matt Thomas (Child's World)

Singapore Sketchbook: The Restoration of a City. Gretchen Liu (Tuttle)

Tales from the Islands of Singapore. Ron Chandran-Dudley (Select Books)

Videos

Exotic Far East. (Rand McNally)

Fodor's Video: Singapore. (IVN Entertainment)

Singapore. Travel Preview series. (Education 2000)

Singapore: Crossroads of Asia. Video Visits series. (IVN Entertainment)

Web Sites

www.att.virtualclassroom.org/vc98/ vc_53/sin_history/ne2.html

www.sg/kids

www.travelforkids.com/Funtodo/ Singapore/singapore.htm

www.zoo.com.sg

Due to the dynamic nature of the Internet, some web sites stay current longer than others. To find additional web sites, use a reliable search engine with one or more of the following keywords to help you locate information about Singapore. Keywords: *Bukit Timah, Elizabeth Choy, Elgin Bridge, Sir Thomas Stamford Raffles, shophouses.*

Index